REQUIEM FOR RHODESIA

Carlos Whitlock Porter

REQUIEM FOR RHODESIA
by Carlos Whitlock Porter

(c) 2015 by Carlos Whitlock Porter. All rights reserved.

http://www.cwporter.com

Cartoon by A. Wyatt Mann.
Used by permission of Tom Metzger,
P.O. Box 401 Warsaw, Indiana 46581
tm_metzger@yahoo.com

Table of Contents

Requiem for Rhodesia 4

Bibliography 35

Epilogue... 37

Requiem for Rhodesia

> Urge neither charity nor shame to me:
> Uncharitably with me have you dealt,
> And shamefully by you my hopes are butcher'd.
>
> – Shakespeare.

> I have set my life upon a cast,
> And I will stand the hazard of the die.
>
> – Shakespeare.

The Rhodesian Railways train stops for water in the desert. Crowds of ragged Africans mob the train, running hysterically to any white face in the window. "Please one penny, *baasjie* (bossie), please give me just one penny", whimpers a filthy child with a swollen belly and bony limbs, barely old enough to walk. Someone throws him a coin. He is beaten viciously and the penny snatched.

In the distance stand thousands of windowless tin shacks, like tool sheds, against a boiling plain after a freezing night; this is a government housing project. Hundreds of other shacks built of trash, paper, and bits of tin, have rocks on the roof to keep them from blowing away. No visible paved roads; few roads of any kind. Scores of teenage prostitutes and hoodlums lounge amongst the filth, coming on board the train to use the toilets. Trash everywhere. Not a white man in sight. Is this Rhodesia?

No. This is Botswana, Black Africa.

Bush, desert, now trees, an unchanging landscape of monotony and misery.

Suddenly a modern gasoline station appears: like a laboratory experiment showing the effect of an invisible line drawn on a map. Suddenly the roads are paved; the Africans are well dressed and muscular, walking about seemingly unconcerned. No shacks. No trash. No begging.

This is Plumbtree. A sign appears:

YOU ARE NOW ENTERING RHODESIA

This is where blacks come illegally in search of work. This is where they are deported.

Border inspection. The train proceeds. Another day, another night. More distance. It takes time to cross Rhodesia. It is not a small country. It is the size of Texas.

A train passes. The 3rd and 4th class carriages are crammed with Africans, lighting fires, hanging out the windows and doors, climbing onto the roof, drinking and shouting. They vanish in a cloud of coal smoke.

In the luxurious dining carriage among a discreet tinkling of silver and rustling of starched linen, a well dressed African is enjoying *truite à la meunière*, shouting to his white travelling companion in a husky, deafening voice.

Africans can travel with you, but you cannot travel with them. Their passage is only a few cents.

Afternoon: Bulawayo. Once the busiest railroad yard in Africa, the spot where Cecil Rhodes took the country away from a chap called Lobengula. It is generally implied that the country belonged to him. It did not. *Bulawayo* means "place of killing" or "place of slaughter". The slaughter, that is, of those who lived here before Lobengula arrived.

A four-hour wait between trains is long enough to see the finest botanical gardens and Natural History Museum in Rhodesia. A mob of Africans from a cement plant passes without a glance, chattering lustily.

The trains are steam, cowboy style. There is no oil in Rhodesia, but there is coal. When UDI (Unilateral Declaration of Independence) and the sanctions came, the brand-new Diesels were traded to South Africa.

Bordered on the north by the Zambezi, which is full of crocodiles, and on the South by the "great grey-green, greasy, Limpopo River", which is dry and full of rocks (at any rate, it *was* when I saw it; or perhaps I was misinformed), Rhodesia lives under a permanent Arab-style oil embargo. The difference is that they are used to it.

This is not the Africa of the movies. This looks like California before the people arrived: wide blue sky in all directions, full of constantly rolling clouds, the hills fading away into the blue of the distance. In the east are mountains and cliffs with very low temperatures. Here life has a Wild West quality, with shooting every week. Here it is still possible but unwise to doze off to sleep under a sign reading: "Beware of Crocodiles". It is dry and hot with heavy thundershowers.

The train squeals to a stop in pitch darkness. There are no lights, no town for miles. A single African gets off the train among the cornfields and trees. He is wearing a white shirt and carrying a suitcase. A quarter of a mile away flickers a single campfire.

* * *

Salisbury, 7:00 A.M. Hundreds of Africans swarm off the trains, loaded down with baggage. Four or five white railroad officials stand around in white uniforms. If you are afraid of colored people, you had better stay home.

Salisbury is pronounced "Sauls-bry", not "Sal-is-berry". Wages are low and prices are high. It is one of the only two countries in the world which declared their independence from Britain illegally. The other one is having a holiday this year – the United States, celebrating the 200th anniversary of its own UDI. (The article was written in 1976 – *Editor's Note*.)

Is there apartheid in Rhodesia? No.

You can go to the Queen's Hotel and listen to rock music with African prostitutes; the Rhodesians are very proud of the Queen's Hotel because they think it is just like America.

You can wait behind Africans in the post office. You can marry an African if you get permission. You can drink with Africans, even though normally they will not drink with you; there is a hotel between Stanley and Speke Streets in Salisbury, with a European bar on Stanley and an African bar on Speke. European means white, even if you are Japanese. They are not labeled: if you should happen to enter the African bar, you will simply be told that your bar is around the corner. It is extremely difficult to mistake them, since the African bars are so much noisier.

The bars follow English pub hours, which means it is impossible to get a drink between 2:30 and 5:30 in the hot afternoons. There are those who would consider this a far greater nuisance than any amount of so-called discrimination.

The University of Rhodesia at Salisbury is 50% African; in 1973 it was 10%, but due to excrement in the showers and other complaints the opinion became widespread that you had to go to South Africa to get a good education.

You cannot, however, go to the largest (and one of the best) sports arenas in Rhodesia; that is reserved for non-whites only.

Salisbury has a lot of trees, wide streets, whitewashed bungalows with tin roofs covered by jacaranda, a park and town square, a stone cathedral. Salisbury radio alternates between English and Mashona news broadcasts and music. Mashona music sounds vaguely similar to the bossa nova or calypso. Most of the police one sees are Africans; they ride around on bicycles and carry a little billy club about eight inches long. White police are not seen very often and normally do not carry guns. Pistol permits are not easy to get.

It is usually quite easy to tell when your house has been burglarized by an African. They cover up all the mirrors with towels to prevent an image being held and betraying them to the police. On one occasion an African broke into a man's house and killed him and stole his clothes. The next day he was arrested walking up and down the street right outside. He was quite indignant when arrested because the witch doctor had given him something to make him invisible.

The way to protect yourself is to get a big dog with a loud bark. However, it is best not to become too attached to him as he will probably eventually be poisoned.

You will never see a dog catcher in Rhodesia. Stray dogs are eaten.

It is common to see the witch doctors selling twigs and bits of bone and other organic material from blankets spread out on the sidewalks even in the very large towns. They shop for *material medica* in the drugstores. They stick something in their hair that looks like mud and hang little bits that look like monkey testicles all about them.

"Sure, maybe the Europeans can cure you better than the witch doctor, but they will never be able to tell you who gave you the disease."

When I was in Rhodesia one of the witch doctors became converted to Christianity and wrote a book detailing the secrets of his trade. For appendicitis he would take a lump of hair or bone in his mouth, make a cut with a razor blade, suck blood, spit out the bone and pronounce the operation a success.

An African will go to the hospital, but even an educated one will visit the witch doctor first. It is impossible to overestimate the power of psychosomatic suggestion on an African. If he is told that he will wake up next week with a paralyzed arm, he will wake up next week with a paralyzed arm. If he is told that he will die next week, he will lie down next week and die, if he is sufficiently frightened. A policeman told me that his grandfather had succeeded in murdering a troublesome African on his farm simply by convincing the man that he would die as predicted by a vision. The man obligingly proceeded to do just that. I am not sure I believe this, but I believe it is possible.

Even educated Africans believe in the *tikolosh* (I am sorry to say that I do not know how to spell it). This is an invisible little African boogie man capable of taking over men's bodies and doing great evil.

He is a little short fellow and cannot climb very high, so all your servants must have their beds put up on stilts from time to time. Branches rubbing on a tin roof at night (Africans do not like trees very much) can terrify your servants into quitting, so you must put a pair of scissors under the bed.

A common punishment for minor offences used to be to put the miscreant in a dark cell and tell him there was a *tikolosh* inside. By morning he is scared to death: he has *seen* that *tikolosh*. No more trouble out of him.

Once a man committed fifteen murders and pled not guilty on the grounds that the *tikolosh* did it. A group of educated factory workers in Johannesburg in 1954 dismembered and ate a nun who had nursed them most of her life. A Portuguese doctor was killed for his shiny tools and certificate to practice medicine by a boy he had raised as his own child.

It is difficult to get inside the mind of an African. He has his own way of life: he has lived it for 10,000 years. You cannot enter into it, you cannot understand it. It involves witchcraft, it involves torture. It does not involve voting.

Many Africans do not understand money. There is no "pass system" in Rhodesia, and nothing to prevent the blacks from leaving the *kraals* (villages) and flocking to the cities, where there is not enough work for them and they sleep in vacant lots. Traditionally, money is cattle, wives and children. Wives are purchased from their fathers for "bride price" – usually one cow. Work is for women and slaves. Children keep the cattle. Men fight.

Men walk in front, carrying a stick or umbrella; these are weapons. The women follow: one baby in front and another on their backs, wrapped up and tied down with towels, bobbing along in perfect comfort, one more by each hand, and three suitcases or an enormous bundle balanced on their heads. African babies never cry. A family of seven is perfectly silent. Africans have the same effect on European babies as well: an African can get instant silence from a screaming, sobbing child just by wagging a finger (and cramming a biscuit in his mouth).

Unfortunately you cannot say to an individual fresh from the *kraal*: "Here is a hundred dollars. Find an apartment, get medical insurance, get a check book and figure your balance, and oh yes, fill out these tax forms."

Salisbury is supposed to have more swimming pools per capita than any American city. I never saw a swimming pool anywhere in Rhodesia. Who could afford one? Go to Rhodesia and try to find a job.

How many times will you be told, "Why should I hire you when I can hire an African for a quarter as much?"

But with this difference: the average wage for a white man when I was there was 150 Rhodesian dollars a month, then about 300 American dollars; not much. But it costs 150 Rhodesian dollars a month to rent a house. An African could earn 10 dollars a week and rent a house, which was in many cases almost identical, from the government for 10 dollars a month. You are always hearing about their low wages, but you never hear about what they get for free. There are African, Asian, "colored", and European areas in Salisbury itself, which you cannot tell apart without looking at the people – attractive modern bungalows, some with cars parked outside, with the victims of oppression chatting casually in the front gardens. Whether or not these are a showcase I don't know, but I can tell you they are resented by Rhodesian taxpayers.

Life is a constant struggle for the white Rhodesians, who must work nine hours a day, husband and wife, to keep ahead of the Africans, who are constantly learning new skills and moving into new jobs. Food, beer and cigarettes are cheap, but manufactured items are fantastically expensive.

As they struggle to save, they see the African renting the best house he's ever had from the government for a week's wages; paying no income taxes; doing no compulsory military service; getting free medical care in modern hospitals; paying at the most a few cents for travel, concerts, sports events; packing the house with relatives; putting his wife to work in the garden; growing his own food and tobacco; brewing his own beer; sitting in the sun smoking cigarettes and saving his money to buy a bicycle. And all this with only one of them working!

This is in contrast to the propaganda picture which shows the bloated whites lounging around the swimming pools enjoying the semi-slavery of the starving blacks who spend all their time shouting "Zimbabwe, we want out country", and who, of course, are just like white people except for the color of their skin. Could it be that we have been misinformed?

Could it be that we have been misinformed by the same people who told us that the Viet Cong were not Communist; then, that they Communist, but not backed by Hanoi; that they were backed by Hanoi, but that Hanoi had no troops in the south; that they had troops in the south, but that if we stopped the bombing they would negotiate; that they were not negotiating, but that if we ever did reach an agreement they would respect it; that if we withdrew our troops the war would end; that the war was continuing, but that Hanoi was not taking over the south; that Hanoi was taking over the south, but that none of the other "dominoes" would follow; that the other "dominoes" were following, but that there would be no bloodbath; that there was a bloodbath, but that it did not really matter very much anyhow, etc.

These are the past judgments of people who are now telling us what to do about Rhodesia. Are these honest mistakes?

Africans work long hours, but they are not generally expected to work hard. It is more common to see one or two at work, and four or five asleep. On one occasion Africans were photographed asleep in a park in South Africa. This was shown on television in Britain saying that they had been killed by the police.

Many people hesitate to pay higher wages on the grounds that the more you pay them, the longer they stay drunk; on a typical weekend in Johannesburg or Cape Town, for example, Africans will drink as much as 20,000 gallons of beer and there will be between four and five hundred stabbings.

However, I did know one "boy" named George whom I considered genuinely exploited by an extremely unpleasant woman named Mrs. Timms, because she cheated all the white people as well. We all hated her. Anyhow, George worked 10 hours a day, 28 days a month, for 10 Rhodesian dollars a month. Since the average is about 10 hours a day, six days a week, for about 40 a month, I asked him one time, "Hey George, why don't you quit?" He said, "Oh well, I have a wife and two children, and if I quit I'd be unemployed for 2 or 3 months." Of course, I was completely stupefied with amazement that he could support a wife and two children on 10 dollars a month, but he said, "Oh yes, she lives in the *kraal* and grows all her own food; I only send five home".

These Africans did not particularly like meat; George and the boys could have all the beef, chicken, lamb or pork they wanted, more than they could eat. The stuff was thrown away because it only cost about fifteen Rhodesian cents a pound. They told me they preferred mealy-meal, a kind of mush. Africans are supposed to have no heart disease or cancer if they don't eat our food, though they don't know this.

I know another African in Johannesburg who got together with his relatives and bought a brand-new van for cash; he used to pick up his employer and charge him a fortune to take him around town. Poor old Billy (the employer) lived in an old busted down dump with damp walls (in Johannesburg, which is notoriously dry), and drove an old clunker. This was the owner of an established piano business left him by his father, and he was convinced his employees lived better than he did.

Cars are scarce in Rhodesia, where a cheap second hand one costs between one and two thousand Rhodesian dollars, but the percentage of car ownership (cash down) is higher among South African blacks than it is in the Soviet Union.

An average sized restaurant in Rhodesia may have up to ten waiters. If their wages were not low, nobody would hire them, because you have to go right back to the beginning with an African.

"You tell him what to do," said a railroad switchman, "and you say, do you understand me, and he says yes, and the next thing you know he's lying there dead. You can never be sure they understand you."

Africans are different; they are also different from each other. Every tribe has its distinct personality and characteristics. They may look alike to us, but not to each other.

At a dance, one tribe will get up and dance, the other will sit down; half the audience will smile and joke, and other half will not. These are different tribes. If you build a township for one tribe, they will not tolerate members of other tribes living there. They will not tolerate members of other related tribes from different parts of Rhodesia, Zambia or Mozambique living there. They will not dance together; they will not sit together; they will not talk to each other; they will not intermarry; they will not work together without frequent killing.

In South West Africa an ordinance was passed allowing hotels and restaurants to serve blacks if they wished (apartheid is largely a matter of local ordinance). Well-dressed Africans began to appear outside. Some were served, some were not. Fifteen hundred of those who were not, apparently just because they found themselves in the same place at the same time, collected on opposite sides of a road and began to fight with each other. They fought for three days with spears and rocks. That ordinance was scrapped.

These disturbances, which occur spontaneously, are called "faction fights".

"Africa is the most racist country on earth," an African medical student studying in Spain told me once. "I come from a little country about this big [indicating a coffee cup] – Spanish Guinea, Equatorial Guinea". He began naming regions in his country. "The people from the mountains hate the people from the jungles, the people from the jungles hate the people from the plains, the people from the plains hate the people from the coast, the people from the countryside hate the people from the cities, the people in the cities hate everybody... what can you do?"

Colonial history has been somewhat peculiarly distorted. The British were invited into Zambia to protect the inhabitants from the

Matabele, and entered East Africa to destroy the Arab slave trade. Perhaps those vociferous African converts to Mohammedanism would be amused to find themselves in the hands of an Islamic specialist in the castration of Negroes to be sold as harem guards.

All African countries are fictitious entities created by drawing lines on maps in Europe, without regard to tribal boundaries, loyalties, or hatreds, and can only be held together by dictatorship (more fashionably called "one party government"). Tribes are cut in half by lines on maps they have never seen. It is to be expected that Africans understand their own people better than we do, and are considerably crueler with them. But it is not they who get the blame.

It is commonly alleged in order to excuse the excesses of African dictatorships such as Mobutu's, that Africans despise any form of weakness and that well-intentioned generosity will be interpreted as such. That is equally true of white-ruled states as well. It is well-known that to this day the most respected colonists of Cameroon, South West Africa and Tanzania were the Germans, because they were the strictest and most rigid.

Reporters who visit the white-rule states think they know better than the people who live there. At one time this would have been called "prejudice". Such people know all the facts except the obvious ones, and constantly pretend that if Africans were treated as something which they are not, Africa would be as democratic as Switzerland. The truth is that Africans will not share power with each other, much less with you, and such theorists are seldom willing to invest their own lives and property in the experiment.

"It's meaningless to talk about prejudice," said an English immigrant to South Africa. "Prejudice means pre-judging, it means forming an opinion in the absence of facts... expressing an opinion when you don't know what you are talking about." He shrugged. "If a Zulu girl wanted to marry a Xhosa man or vice versa, their parents would kill them, they'd kill both of them. But... that's not prejudice, that's just a fact of life. If you're a Zulu and she's a Xhosa, you just bloody well don't get married!"

Rhodesia has segregated schools. Whites are fee-paying, black schools are free; the whites pay twice, tuition and tax as well. Blacks are educated separately from each other. Why not? Every time you put them together, they kill each other.

It is also because the Africans have no mutually intelligible language, apart form English, which they have to learn. It is impossible to imagine how basic their education must be. Many of them have never seen a table, a chair, a stairway, a handkerchief or a toilet. They must be taught to think in an entirely different way: for instance, there is a tribe in Angola who use a compound word for "seven" which means, literally, "six plus two"! They do not need intellectuals. They need basic skills. An intellectual cannot make a living in rural America. How many can Black Africa absorb?

"Help me haul wood," said Albert Schweitzer. – "I do not haul wood. I am in intellectual." – "You are very lucky. I tried to be an intellectual, but did not succeed."

Africans have no tradition of private property. Your servants will take one tea bag, one sheet, one shirt, out of every four; your wrist watch; your alarm clock. "I'm not angry, John, but I know you took this..." – "No, no, *baasjie*, I didn't..." It is not stealing. "Africans were socialists before the invention of the word," said the black Prime Minister of Tanzania.

Yes, and if a primitive system of economics means a primitive standard of living, why, the difference must be made up by a white man. This is why nearly every single Black African country pursues a socialist economy under Russian or Chinese influence, receiving capitalist foreign aid.

The Congo, Brazzaville, which was one of the first countries in Africa to be given its independence on a silver platter, is almost as Communist as Angola, which fought for it for thirteen years.

The two countries in Africa where blacks were happiest and best treated were, according to John Gunther, Uganda and the Belgian Congo. The model for independent Africa was Nigeria. The two countries with no color bar, where intermarriage was officially encouraged and mulattoes were officially considered white, were Mozambique and Angola.

You cannot change an African for the better by the way you treat him; only for the worse.

There are two main tribes in Rhodesia: the Mashona and the Matabele. The Mashona live around Salisbury, and the Matabele live further south, around Bulawayo.

Amashuna is a Matabele word meaning "dog" or "servile person". The Mashona are cheerful, sociable people. You will often see three or four ice cream vendors together on the same street corner, as they would rather enjoy company than compete for business. They love band uniforms and shiny instruments. But if the director is not looking for a moment, they are certain to begin punching each other and giggling or chasing each other around. You often see them playing pranks on each other, such as twisting each other's arms. If they see you watching and enjoying the joke, they break out in spontaneous grins. Their language sounds like Brazilian.

The Matabele are an offshoot of the Zulu tribe which moved into South Africa several hundred years ago killing off the bushmen and other tribes. The Matabele are mean-looking, do not smile very often, and walk with a slight swagger. Their language sounds like Japanese. Personally I do not care for the Matabele, even though I do not mind the Zulus.

The African regiment of the Rhodesian Army is called the Rhodesian African Rifles, divided up into Mashona and Matabele regiments. When there is trouble in the Matabele areas of Rhodesia, the Mashona troops are sent. When there is trouble in the Mashona area, the Matabele troops are sent. The results are sometimes too horrible for words.

Africans have no tradition of political voting. They may or may not choose their own chief, but after that they will ask him how to vote and they will all vote that way. Another fount of political wisdom is the witch doctor. Consequently it is a matter of great importance to the terrorists and Smith government to have the chiefs and witch doctors on their side.

All politics in Africa is tribal. Politics, religion, color, are just new names. Parties are organized along tribal lines. If two tribes are enemies (and they are nearly all enemies), and one fights for the terrorists, the others will either fight for the whites or form their own "terr" groups and fight each other. The three Marxist terrorist armies in Angola reported each other's troop movements to the Portuguese for years. The *Frente Nacional* (FNLA), for example, was made up of Bakongo tribesmen from across the Angola-Congo (Zaire) border, and was later backed by that country in its civil war against the *Movimento Popular* (MPLA) and the *União Nacional* (UNITA). These others had been geographical and tribal enemies of the Bakongos for years.

Mozambique had two main tribes, the Macua and the Makonde (I am sorry to say I don't remember which is which). One lived on both sides of the Tanzanian border and made up the main forces of the *Frelimo* (*Frente de Liberacão de Moçambique*) terrorists. The others, two million strong, fought for the Portuguese and made up 60% of their army. When "independence" came, they asked *Frelimo* for elections and were told politely to go to hell. Where is all the talk about stopping Communism by satisfying the "legitimate aspirations" of these people?

In Rhodesia there are two main terrorist groups following the same pattern.

It is useless to wait for "education" to detribalize the Africans. Tribe is as fundamental as nation, language, religion, culture. The only detribalized Africans in the world are the descendents of the New World slaves. Uprooted by force; deliberately mixed; taught an alien language; dumped on the other side of the world for two centuries; outnumbered and educated by whites – how else could it be done? The New World Negroes are the only ones born speaking a common language (English, Spanish or Portuguese). They are the only ones who accept the racially mixed as belonging to their own race.

The African "colored" (with European, Indian, Malay, Hottentot or Chinese ancestry) belongs to no tribe, is accepted nowhere, has no culture of his own, and has a significantly higher rate of social problems than the African. This is one reason why interracial sex was made a criminal offence in South Africa.

It is not generally known that Mahatma Gandhi began his career as a nationalistic agitator among the Indians of South Africa. Unlike Mr. Gandhi himself, these poor fellows are almost black in color, since *varna* – caste – means "color". These descendants of voluntarily contracted railway and plantation workers are (or were) found in large numbers all over former British East Africa, and have a reputation for Communism in politics, as well as for extreme dishonesty in business dealings. They buy up reject shirts for next to nothing and sell them to the Africans on pay day for many times the price of a good one. The Africans know they are being cheated but continue to buy from them. Africans are paid in services more than money partly to protect them from precisely this type of exploitation.

South Africa spent fifty years trying to pay the Indians to go home, but could not get them to leave. Every one who did compared the freedom and opportunities in India and wrote advising his friends and relatives to stay put.

Apparently it requires the vigor of an African to accomplish that at which the whites have tried and failed. "Majority rule" in most African countries to date has simply meant that when the expropriation and expulsion of whites have been completed, the Asians will suffer the same; followed by the murder of the racially mixed and smaller tribes, resulting in a dictatorship of the tribe with the most foreign aid from Russia or China; then comes foreign aid from Britain and America.

Critics of racial separation stress its discriminatory aspects while ignoring the practical reasons for its existence. Port Shepstone, South Africa, had a very high burglary rate. An ordinance was passed making it illegal for blacks to be in town past eight o'clock at night. The burglary rate fell to zero.

One has to live in these countries to experience the relaxed racial atmosphere which normally prevails in contrast to comparable areas of America. It is common even in "tension-ridden" Johannesburg to chat with an African on a street corner over "whose bus will come first – yours or mine?" Since there are more buses for Africans than for whites, it is usually yourself who waves goodbye and continues to wait.

I walked all over Johannesburg and Cape Town at night and passed thousands of Africans who ignored me completely. The Johannesburg Star printed a front-page article about a white man who was knocked down and robbed of five Rand (then US $6.50) by an African; the same when some women had their purses snatched. Perhaps those same wonderful people who brought you the larger American cities should cease to export what does not work at home.

Southern African justice is a matter of mandatory minimum sentencing imposed according to evidence. Social revolution, omniscience, and personal whim are left to the politicians.

The system of townships and tribal lands in Rhodesia is in fact no different from the system of Indian reservations in America (apart from the missing element of broken treaties, deportations, massacres and lynchings). The system of independent tribal homelands in South Africa is in fact identical to those "black republics" once demanded by American black radicals. The latter are the only areas in the world where blacks can rule free from the conflicting and sometimes violent ambitions of other races and tribes.

However, even these areas, set up and educated for responsible democratic government by the South African government at great expense, reject democracy and voting at the first available opportunity to do so. In one of these states, the first royal act of King Jonathan, "the world's longest reigning monarch", who had ruled his people longer than Queen Victoria had ruled hers, was to abolish Parliament, outlaw the opposition parties, and declare a dictatorship within several days of independence. The first act of independent Ovamboland was to institute public floggings. The world protested and blamed South Africa. South Africa asked them to stop it. They replied that they were independent now, it was a tribal custom, and they could do what they liked.

Yet African agitators demand the vote in Rhodesia. The agitators have it already, since most of them are educated; they wish the vote so as to get themselves into office to declare a dictatorship of their own.

A leader of the Rhodesian African nationalists in London has declared that "majority" rule for Rhodesia will involve no pretense at parliamentary government. It will be the usual dictatorship of a self-appointed minority.

Relations between Rhodesia and South Africa are not what you would expect. This is partly because the founder of Rhodesia tried to overthrow the government of what is today South Africa. Britain declared war on the Boer Republics because English gold seekers in the Transvaal, an independent foreign country, were not allowed to vote on the grounds that they outnumbered the inhabitants. The Boers (Afrikaans-speaking whites) are not cruel people; British prisoners of war were released unharmed to walk back to their lines minus boots and trousers. By contrast the British interned all women and children in concentration camps where 25,000 of them died of disease. World opinion was on the side of the Boers. Today the Boers control the country and have little use for the British or for world opinion. The British consider Africans their equals and the Boers their inferiors. The Boers consider Africans primitive and the English effete.

Another reason is that both countries talked tough while Portugal did all the fighting, and are now trying to buy time.

White Rhodesians are not racists. They are engaged in a highly idealistic experiment (an unrealistic one, in my opinion). They are convinced that an educated African will think and vote like an educated white man instead of like a black nationalist; that when all men are educated, their interests do not conflict. They believe (or used to believe) that their generosity would be recognized by the world.

I believe that common observation shows nothing could be further from the truth on both points. The average uneducated African is unemployed, has six or eight children, and is sharing everything with his relatives. He is not interested in politics. He wants the whites to stay because he wants a job, which he knows can only be supplied directly or indirectly by the whites. He wants to buy a bicycle, a new shirt, and a new pair of shoes. He does not want to be murdered en masse by members of another tribe. He does not want to be paralyzed by having a sharpened bicycle spoke jabbed in his spine. An African wrote to me in England and said, "As you know, Mozambique is in the hands of Africans, and the future for us Rhodesians is very uncertain."

An educated African, unless he is a doctor, knows that in a European-dominated society the most he can aspire to is a teaching position; kick out the whites, and he can be Prime Minister (with a chalet and bank account in Switzerland), marry a white woman and live in a palace. This is not a fantasy. Ability is no object. African countries take a man who was cleaning toilets, and make him a bank president from one day to the next.

This is the African who goes about promising his fellows that when the Europeans are expelled, all Africans will drive cars. This is the

African who promises UN posts to illiterates. This is the African who goes on speaking tours in Europe and is interviewed by the world's journalists.

In Malawi the word for "politician" is *Wa-Benz*. *Wa* is "man", and *Benz*, of course, is Mercedes-Benz.

In 1972 the British government sent a commission to Rhodesia to arrange an African vote on Rhodesian independence. These people dedicated themselves to going about the countryside finding illiterates and asking them whether they thought Rhodesia should be a republic or not. They published their itinerary in advance.

Consequently an organization known as the African National Congress always managed to get there "firstest with the mostest" in an effort to intimidate African voting. This organization was originally founded in South Africa many years ago, became a Communist front in 1941, and was banned by the Smith government as a terrorist organization. Later it was resurrected to negotiate for the Africans in the so-called "constitutional talks". It was in this case a simple matter for the ANC to intimidate their fellows by talking of hut burning, beating, and the like, even though they were few in number. Since the whites were all voting yes, a vote of no was considered a victory for the British government and African nationalists.

300 Africans working in one factory were all going to vote yes. The next day they all came in and voted no.

I was lucky to work in Rhodesia because I am a piano tuner and Africans cannot be taught to tune; they have a different sense of pitch. For instance, there is only one African piano tuner in all of Zambia and he could not raise pitch if he had to. However, they can do everything else if you teach them how: regulate, rebuild, restring, French polish, etc.

A friend of mine named Jimmy Eschelby had a piano shop called Smith and Hall, Pioneer St. Salisbury, with a staff of about 10 skilled piano technicians who had been working with him for 12 years. One day they came to him with a question: how should they vote? He said, "Well, I'm not supposed to tell you that; you're supposed to figure that out for yourselves." But they insisted, so he said to one of them, "Look, how many children do you have?" I forget what it was, six or eight. "Well, the oldest one's getting out of school next year, isn't he, what's he going to do, has he got a job yet?" No, he hadn't.

"Well," said, Jimmy, "look, if we can get a settlement, the money will pour into Rhodesia, I can expand my business and hire more help." (The sanctions were costing him a thousand Rhodesian dollars a month in lost profit and Rhodesia has unexploited resources of virtually every known mineral.) Well, that was good enough. They were all going to vote yes.

A little while later they were back: "Was it true that there was an invisible man in the polling booth who would tell on them if they voted yes?" They voted no.

Rhodesians are different. They love Rhodesia. Everything is always bigger, better, cheaper and more wonderful in Rhodesia. They are the world's biggest optimists. Typically they believe anything is easy until they get into it, and then they tend to get bogged down. But they never give up. They will not give up over a conference table everything they could lose in a war.

One day I went to visit somebody sick in Salisbury Hospital. The place was full of soldiers; there had just been an ambush. "Any of them hurt bad?" I asked. – "That one over there is. He's lost a couple of legs." The boy was about nineteen and was whispering to his girlfriend, "I've been to funerals of friends of mine killed by terrorists, and tourists come down here having a good time and tell us how we're mistreating the blacks."

They do not worry about the terrorism. They prepare for it. In the war zones they take an automatic rifle to the golf course and come back before dark.

One day we went out to deliver a piano to a farm that belonged to the daughter of the Rhodesian Minister of Defense. It was out in the bush and had about 30 Africans working on it. The roads were all full of dirt and lined with brush. "We'll get around to paving them all one of these days," said my companion cheerfully. "It makes it more difficult to put land mines in them."

Another time I paid a few dollars to go up in a private plane and have a look at Vic Falls, one the biggest in the world, with a fantastic series of rapids, switchbacks, and sheer cliffs. When we were about a thousand feet in the air over the middle of the river, the pilot remarked casually that it might not be a good idea to go too close to the other side.

"Oh really, why not?" – "Oh well, it seems the Zambian army killed three tourists yesterday, and we might get shot down."

These tourists came from my hotel and were having a picnic on the Rhodesian side in their bathing suits. Two were killed immediately by machine gun fire from the Zambian side, and the third, one of the girls, hid behind a rock for half an hour waist deep in the crocodile-infested water until they moved the guns and killed her. The body was never found.

The Zambians accused them of trying to swim across to their side of the river to blow up a power station. Sure. Through forty-nine million gallons of water a minute rushing through a narrow gorge and the shallows full of crocs.

These teenagers were American and Canadian, but no note of protest was ever forthcoming to the Zambian government because of it. It was Rhodesia's fault for creating tension in the area, and the Americans should not have been there. (I believe it was in Uganda about eight years ago that two American newspaper reporters were killed and fed to crocs for witnessing the murder of an entire army barracks. The American government demanded an investigation and was perfectly satisfied when the chief suspect was placed in charge.)

What if the Rhodesian Army had killed Americans having a picnic in Zambia?

It was in connection with this incident that Ian Smith said, *"If your skin is black, you will be forgiven anything."*

Do you doubt this? Let me quote from *Time Magazine*, November 5, 1965, a week before UDI:

"Even in the bloody Congo, Belgians blame themselves for much of the chaos and exonerate the Congolese for the slaughters that followed independence, on the grounds that it was nothing more than tribal ebullience – long restrained by Belgian rule – expressing itself at the agitation of the Communists."

This is the gulf between Rhodesia and the world.

What would they say if every nurse and nun in Rhodesia were suddenly raped by white Rhodesian soldiers?

What would they say if Ian Smith carried a penis impaled on the end of a stick?

What would they say if a Rhodesian Army officer cut out a man's liver and ate it on the runway of Salisbury Airport?

What would they say if Rhodesian blacks were taken to be skinned alive by whites in trucks filled with bicycles, melons and hitchhikers?

What would they say if those very morally superior African students at the University of Rhodesia at Salisbury were to have their fingers cut off because they could write, or were killed because they wore shoes?

Could Ian Smith chop up a child and use the pieces for soccer practice?

Could Ian Smith cut living captives in half lengthwise with buzz-saws, like his supposed "anti-Communist" confreres in Angola?

Could Ian Smith trap 14 million Africans in a tiny corner of jungle and slowly starve them to death, like the Nigerians?

Could the Rhodesian Army disembowel and then rape a pregnant African for an initiation ritual?

Could Rhodesia be allowed to act like any other UN member?

What would it be called? Good clean fun? *Tribal ebullience?* An indigenous local custom of the Rhodesian New Year?

Let us take a look at the map.

UGANDA: Up to a quarter million Africans killed in Britain's former "model colony". – People forced by the army to line up and kill each other in turn. – People forced to eat fried pieces cut from their own bodies. – Monkey meat and ground-nuts on the menus of Africa's ex-finest hotels and restaurants. – A high government official going about chopping off penises with a sword. – Tribes exterminated. – The Asians expelled. – The country's leading citizens kidnapped and killed. – A soccer pitch converted into an execution ground. – Political opponents fed to crocodiles...

Ian Smith is an outlaw.

Idi Amin is the President of the Organization of African Unity: unanimously elected, not once, but twice. Here is the African nationalist's ideal of a perfect African nationalist. This is what they would be if they could. He is invited to New York, and addresses the UN.

But Ian Smith is an outlaw.

CENTRAL AFRICAN REPUBLIC: Legalized mutilation for criminal offences. – Overcrowding in prisons relieved by beating all the prisoners to death. – Compulsory tribal initiation rites written into law by a witch-doctor president. – The country's leading citizens forced to crawl naked through anthills...

EQUATORIAL GUINEA: The robbery and murder of Nigerian contract workers. – The re-legalization of slavery. – 22,000 Africans in forced labor on the cocoa plantations. – The entire literate population in exile...

NIGERIA: Thirty thousand murders in one day starts a two-year civil war costing two million lives. – Africans lured out of the jungle with Red Cross trucks and killed. – Jungle animals inoculated with rabies. – All prisoners of war are shot. – Children nailed up in huts and burned to death or left to starve. – Public executions for criminal offences in peacetime...

RWANDA: One hundred thousand Tutsis (Watusi) killed by their Hutu slaves. – The tall Hamitic Tutsis become as extinct as the dodo in that country...

BURUNDI: One hundred thousand Hutus killed by Tutsis in "kill or be killed" massacre. – Bodies taken away in army trucks to be dumped in the jungle...

LIBERIA: One hundred and forty-year rule of the slave-trading (into the 1930s) Creole descendants of American slaves. – The dark-skinned 99% majority of Africans who originally inhabited the country are despised and have never been allowed to vote...

ZANZIBAR: The entire Arab population of the island massacred with torture after they are caught drunk on a religious holiday...

SENEGAL: A trumped-up invasion by Portuguese soldiers reportedly provides the pretext for boiling political adversaries in oil...

ZAMBIA: All land nationalized. – Real estate offices closed. – Churches abolished. – Mission schools closed. – Canned beans declared a luxury item. – Christian Lumpas exterminated. – No newspapers on Monday if the staff is too drunk to print them...

MOZAMBIQUE: The first officially Communist state in Africa confiscates all private homes and farms, then asks the Rhodesians to feed them. – Families gang-raped and butchered with husbands forced to watch. – The revolutionary Portuguese government claims everything is under control and helps Frelimo round up anti-Communist Portuguese...

KENYA: Mau Mau terrorist Kenyatta wrecks the country's agriculture dividing up European farms into uneconomical plots for the Kikuyu. – The Masai get nothing. – Opposition party politicians are jailed from time to time to remind them that "the hawk is in the sky and ready to swoop down on the chickens". – Kenya thrives under his "free enterprise" dictatorship...

GHANA: "Redeemer" and "Black Christ" Nkhrumah ("Every woman in Ghana is my wife") sets an early record for self-aggrandizement and glorification which holds to this day. – "Clean-up" government campaign deprives opposition members of their seats for absenteeism – of course, they are absent because they are all in jail...

MALAWI: One hundred thousand Jehovah's Witnesses chased into the jungles by Malawi, Zambia and Mozambique. – Men and women tied together with itching beans rubbed into their sexual organs. – People beaten to death with poles or left to starve. – The expulsion of 40,000 Asians begun but not yet completed...

ANGOLA: Holden Roberto's "anti-Communist" *Frente Nacional* starts a 13-year war attacking Luanda with Chinese weapons, infiltrating from the Congo and committing some of the most famous atrocities in Africa, the dismemberments by buzz-saw. – The Portuguese begin doing four years military service as the poorest nation in Europe fights the entire Communist world and Scandinavia for colonies 25 times the size of metropolitan Portugal. – Officers conscripted out of the universities create a pro-Communist officer class which overthrows the government. – The "Red Admiral" from Lisbon encourages the Soviet-backed *Movimento Popular* to re-arm and attack the homes of "fascistic" European settlers who built the first modern city in Western Africa. – Roberto's tribesmen begin hiring mercenaries and are backed by South Africa, in a monumental error of judgment, presumably because the Soviets have a navy but the Chinese do not. – A year-long civil war fought mainly on the basis of noise (one side advancing firing wildly and the other getting scared and falling back if they couldn't make as much *espalhafato* – noise) kills few soldiers but 100,000 civilians. – 750,000 Portuguese leave the lands they had colonized when nearly uninhabited and occupied for 500 years, with two suitcases and a handful of money which could not be exchanged in any country. – Unpaid *Movimento Popular* troops celebrate victory with a rampage of looting and killing...

CONGO (Brazzaville): Chinese is made one of the official languages, even though none of the Africans can speak it...

CONGO (Zaire): Four-year civil war full of mass rape, cannibalism, and torture. – 16 Italian Air Force men killed and eaten. – Congolese envoy to the UN killed and eaten, but his briefcase saved. – The only peaceful province invaded and wrecked by mercenary "peace keeping" troops from the UN ("the pay is very good, twice what we get in Sweden"). – A Congolese army officer brutally rapes an English nun, then puts his arm around her tenderly and says, "Now you are my wife." She is saved from death by torture by white mercenaries from Rhodesia (it is not generally known that one in five of these was killed and very few ever got paid for saving so many lives)...

SUDAN: A 27-year civil war...

ETHIOPIA: Students blown up with dynamite to save ammunition...

TANZANIA: Another Communist dictatorship which "Africanized" the railroads and wrecked all the trains, then asked the Europeans to come back...

This is *"freedom"*.
There is a 1500-mile long illegal slave trade route in Africa today. There is an Anti-Slavery Society in London. There is an Anti-Slavery Commission in the UN. All the slave-trading countries are UN members.
"Britain has granted independence to more people than any other nation in history," bragged Harold Wilson. – "Yes," said Ian Smith, "and in one instance this resulted in a million people being killed in three days."

INDIA: 10 million peasants thrown onto the roads overnight as Hindus and Moslems fight to kick each other out of what is today India and Pakistan. – Refugee trains stopped en route, and their passengers slaughtered. – Vultures feed on the remains of entire towns massacred by religious bandits. – A later civil war costs two lives in disgusting atrocities...

These are the dictatorial pacifists who lecture the world, and Southern Africa in particular, on peace and love.
Have you heard of our moral obligations imposed on us internationally by the UN? Compare Biafra to East Pakistan. Compare the Congo to Hungary or Prague. Compare Rhodesia to Uganda. Compare Africa to Eastern Europe.
You will see that all UN actions, morals, obligations and commitments are created solely by Soviet interests.
Do you remember when it was "immoral" to import Rhodesian chrome – a vital defense material, essential for high-grade steel, the only decent chrome in the world? (Filipino chrome is no good.) The Rhodesians sold it to the Russians for 35 USD a ton. The Russians sold

it to America for 70 USD a ton. Thus was Rhodesian chrome made "moral". (Source: A.J.A. Peck, *Rhodesia Accuses*.)

In Africa, European-owned farms, homes and businesses are tolerated only until the Africans can stand the chaos created by their confiscation. The owners are given 24 hours to leave the country with two suitcases and a few dollars; or they are given cash and expelled, but are prohibited by "exchange control regulations" from taking the cash with them; or they are paid off with government bonds which do not mature for 25 years and can be repudiated by any succeeding government; or they are terrorized by thugs and are told by the police, "If you don't like it, why don't you get out of the country?" Then technicians are imported to exploit the resources created or discovered by the former whites. Statistics are falsified by equating the old whites with the new ones. *"Despite the horror of the past, there are now 60,000 Belgians (or whatever) spread through the Congo, which once had 90,000, and the nation's industries, commerce and transport system could not work without them."* Ah, but which ones are they?

This is the new colonialism. We must help to kill the white Rhodesians so as to butter up the blacks into allowing us to help exploit their property or the enormous mineral resources which the blacks were never aware of.

"The trouble is, a lot of the Europeans just got greedy," said a woman in Salisbury who ran from Zambia. "A lot of them just thought, 'Oh well, it won't happen to me.' I knew someone who had a business in Zambia. He stayed. They waited ten years. Then, sure enough, when he had built it up into an established business, they 'Africanized' it."

The terrorists are not freedom fighters. To be in the army in Rhodesia is relatively safe unless you happen to step on a landmine, run into an ambush, or catch up with someone you are chasing. Terrorists stay away from soldiers because soldiers carry guns. The purpose of terrorism is to discourage civilian cooperation with an established government. What is not safe is to be an unarmed African in a terrorist-infested zone. Such a person is likely to see his chief beaten to death, his wife and daughters raped, his sons kidnapped, or his ears, lips and nose cut off *"pour encourager les autres"*. He will be told, "We are coming back. Do not tell the Europeans which way we went. We want so many bags of maize waiting for us when we return."

Since he fears being cut to pieces with a rusty bayonet more than he fears hanging or imprisonment at the hands of the authorities, the whites cannot win in a contest of terror and do not try. They are forced to appeal to the African self-interest in some way. Primarily, this means two things: protection and revenge.

One reason so many blacks are killed fighting for the Smith government is because the terrorists will not surrender to them. They know how hated they are. It is a big problem in the Rhodesian army to get the Rhodesian African Rifles to take prisoners.

Terrorists are recruited by kidnapping and disciplined by torture. 400 African children were kidnapped from a mission school and taken towards the Mozambique border with the Army in pursuit. Occasionally the "terrs" will kill a farmer if they can catch him in the field or see him through the windows at night; once in a while they will ambush cars. Recently they tossed a hand grenade into a restaurant, an IRA trick which is as likely to kill some of the over-abundant black waiters as anybody else. But generally, you are far more likely to be killed by a drunken driver on the long empty Rhodesian roads than you are by a terrorist.

The Mau Mau terror in Kenya, for example, killed 13,000 blacks and lasted for years, but killed exactly 55 white soldiers and civilians.

The terrorism has nothing to do with Rhodesia's independence disputes, and began long before. A friend of mine taught at a private school, Cranborne Boys' School in Salisbury with about 200 students. There was a plaque with plenty of space left on it in the chapel, dedicated to students who had been killed on military service in the Zambezi Valley. There were about six of them, going all the way back to the early 1960s.

Is failing to outnumber the blacks really a worse crime than murdering them all? Or is it simply that the Rhodesians are white? Are we fighting a race war against ourselves? Do we despise ourselves that much? Or is it simply that we only care about money?

"Oh God, let my neighbors be slaughtered one by one, let my children live under Communism, but let me have my boat, my car, my TV, my sauna bath, my swimming pool, my plane, but oh God, please don't make me think about tomorrow."

Rhodesia is criticized because the whites hold half the land. Who do you think is going to feed them all? One would think the blacks eradicated sleeping sickness, which made much of the country uninhabitable; one would think it was the witch doctors who allowed their population to increase by a factor of ten in eighty-five years.

Perhaps you have noticed that countries in which Africans hold all the land must subsist largely off foreign aid. The Frelimo government of Mozambique confiscated the homes and farms of a quarter million Portuguese, and then asked the Rhodesians to feed their starving population! As soon as they got their hands on a couple of trainloads of Rhodesian maize, they declared war on Rhodesia! They were instantly given a healthy dose of foreign aid "assistance" by Britain, whose socialist Prime Minister at that time owned five houses.

This is "independent African agriculture". Who is supposed to provide the Africans with all the benefits of civilization which they enjoy but seldom pay for?

What would happen to the standard of living of America and the world if all the best land were divided up into 1-acre parcels to be farmed by people who use no machinery, who plant by poking holes in the ground with a stick, who use no contour plowing or erosion control, no artificial fertilizer, who quit work for several years every time they get a good harvest, who use no crop rotation, or who erode and exhaust the land and then move?

The South African government spent 77 million Rand (100 million dollars) on farm machinery for the Zulus. The next year everything was rusting and going back to bush. And the Africans said, "We had a good harvest last year, why the hell should we work this year?"

Japanese agronomists visited the Transkei, an independent homeland for the Xhosa. They said it could feed three million Oriental peasants and allow them to export food. It cannot feed one million Africans.

Rhodesia is criticized for spending more money on the education of white children than black. What do you expect? The whites are outnumbered every year simply by the number of black babies born. Either the whites must adopt an African standard of culture and educate no one, or they must spend more of their money on themselves.

Half of the blacks in Rhodesia are less than fifteen years old; yet the percentage of population in school is almost as high in Rhodesia as it is in Britain. If the blacks are not capable of educating themselves, what makes them capable of running the country?

American and British policy towards Rhodesia is to support "majority rule", even if that means minorities must be killed. Since this is in direct contradiction to the policies followed in their own countries, where minorities are worshipped, it simply means that if blacks are in the minority, they must be given privileges. If they are not in the minority, they must be given more privileges.

Eighty-five years ago the Rhodesian blacks had no knowledge of the existence of the wheel; today they ride bicycles. Eighty-five years ago they had no written language; today they are taught to read. This is not enough for the world. They must all drive cars and go to university. Who is going to pay for it? Are you?

Eighty-five years ago the Mashona were on the point of extinction at the hands of the Matabele. Today they are in the majority. The general population is ten times what it was. As for "majority rule", if it were not for the whites, there wouldn't be any "majority"; they would all be dead.

There are two terrorist armies in Rhodesia today, divided along the familiar Russian-Chinese, tribal lines, just as there were in Angola. How long will the Mashona enjoy their "rule" when they cease to be protected by the whites?

Perhaps those journalists to whom 10,000 miles' distance has given a superior understanding will explain what gives the African his right to wreck everything. Perhaps those who sell their homes at a loss rather than share a single American city with the blacks will explain whether they would prefer to farm in Zambia.

Perhaps those liberal politicians who force others to integrate, and then send their own children to all-white suburban private schools will explain why the American blacks, who are so much more advanced, ran a convicted rapist (Eldridge Cleaver) for President in 1968, and publicly declared him the "ideal black man", the best they could come up with.

In Belgium and French Canada, say the Rhodesians, people are killed because of linguistic differences. In Northern Ireland, people are killed because of religious differences. In Africa, people are killed because of tribal differences. We have all of that here, and we live in peace. Leave us alone!

To say that one hopes for a peaceful solution to Rhodesia's racial problems while agitating for majority rule is simply to utter a hypocritical threat. Rhodesia's racial problems are created by foreign politicians. If they do not get what they want for nothing, they will resort to war. The peaceful solution is to leave Rhodesia alone.

Do you think that you are generous? Do you want to do right? Would you abandon your home, your business, your savings, risk the lives of your family, to beg charity in foreign countries you have never seen, in climates you have never experienced, in middle age – if you could escape?

And for what? So that Africans can vote? Rhodesia is almost the only country in Africa where they do vote. In the weeks following UDI, military takeovers and revolutions were taking place in Africa at the rate of one a week. Every single one of these dictatorships was recognized by the world within a week.

One man, one vote – one time. When have they voted? Where do they vote? Nowhere but in Rhodesia, the Ivory Coast and Botswana. Botswana is described on page 4 of this book.

Look at the slaughters, look at the tortures, look at the ignorance. It is not enough to treat the Africans better than they have ever treated each other. No. It is not enough to treat the Africans as well as you can.

No. In Rhodesia the rule is not "Do unto others as you would have them do unto you." In Rhodesia the rule must be: "Allow others to do unto you things you would never dream of doing to them, just as long as they are black."

What makes Rhodesia wicked? Let me quote from *Time*, a consistent enemy of Rhodesia:

"The [black population's] standard of living is higher than in any of the black nations to the north... 85 per cent of all school age children are actually in school... there are modern hospitals for blacks in Bulawayo and Salisbury... the townships are neat and well-planned... they compare favorably with the festering shanty towns of Latin America, Asia and other African countries."

Traditional mud hut, replaced by whites in urban areas with attractive modern housing. When I was in Rhodesia, virtually all rural Africans still lived in these structures. This is a Matabele-style hut from the Bulawayo region. As housing, these structures are perfectly adequate: very sturdy, kept very clean, and providing good insulation. Of course, they are not equipped with plumbing or electricity, but what do people expect? This is why many Africans have never seen chairs, tables, toilets, stairways, etc. How is all this "progress" to be produced? With a magic wand?

Everything the Africans have has been given to them by the whites. It is to satisfy the ignorant envy of people too incompetent to supply themselves with the most basic of modern conveniences that Rhodesia must be destroyed. It is to erase the last reminders of their technical and inventive inferiority that the whites must be killed with our help.

"Few of their houses are equipped with electricity," says *Time*. One would think the blacks invented electricity, since it is theirs by right regardless of cost, possibility or birth rates. The whites must be killed to allow the politicians to pretend that they did invent it.

Do you think you are immune? You are next on the list. Do you think the politicians with all their wealth will ever suffer in the world they are creating? They will be in positions of influence and will become richer than ever – like the land-speculating socialist Prime Ministers of Great Britain, or the chauffeured commissars of Soviet Russia with their tax-free salaries, private department stores and reserved freeway lanes.

There are supposed to be 300 American mercenaries fighting in Rhodesia, "with more arriving every day". Do you believe this? The Rhodesian Armed Forces minus reservists, conscripts and Africans amounts to about 1600 men.

To defy the world for independence with a handful of professional soldiers would at one time have been called "courageous". Today that is a privilege reserved "For Non-Whites Only".

Do you remember the famous tank invasion along the Mozambique border, which was expected at any moment? The Mozambique border is made up of 800 miles of 2,000 feet cliffs with few roads. The experts on Rhodesia have never heard of the Zambezi Escarpment. It will remain a guerrilla war for a long time.

Do you remember the famous "Wiriyamu Massacre"? Where Portuguese soldiers were supposed to have killed 400 (or was it 463?) villagers in a village by that name? No village with that or any similar name in that area was ever proven to exist. Yet the stories of the Wiriyamu massacre and the search for the village of Wiriyamu made headlines all over the world for months. (Strangely enough, until the revolution in Portugal almost to the day.) This story was later found to have been fabricated at a conference in Czechoslovakia. About the best thing you can say for newspapers is that they will print anything that makes money.

I repeat that prejudice means pre-judging. It does not mean generalizing on the basis of statistics or experience, because there is no other way to live.

Some people, however, prefer to imitate the joke:

"I know nothing about it and so am completely unprejudiced."

Recently an un-elected American official (Henry Kissinger), without the knowledge or consent of the American people, attempted to commit his adopted country to the support of several unelected Communist dictatorships in their voting-rights war against Rhodesia, a country which that official has never even visited.

Since Mr. Kissinger is a refugee from Nazi Germany, it is apparent that he feels something less than grateful: Rhodesia had the highest killed-in-action ratio of any Commonwealth country during WWII.

Rhodesia would accept Mr. Kissinger; Rhodesia would protect his life, his family, his property and his religion; it would allow him full citizenship after two years.

Can he say the same for Zambia or Mozambique, where religious minorities are tortured, killed or driven into the jungles to starve, where churches are abolished, and where religion is illegal?

Neither has there ever been any anti-Semitic legislation in South Africa, where Jews enjoy full political rights.

South African Jews are among the richest in the world. They are the second greatest single source of Israeli foreign exchange. They have been allowed to do this in a very short time. And they have almost single-handedly financed the movement towards black rule in that country. They are also known to pay or treat their Africans no better than anyone else, as personal experience and strikes at Mr. Oppenheimer's diamond company can soon attest.

Somehow such people as Mr. Kissinger never manage to give away anything which belongs to them personally. *"Tis thine they give away, and not their own. Pirates may make cheap penny-worths of their pillage, and purchase friends, and give to courtesans, still reveling, like lords, till all be gone; whileas the silly owner of the goods weeps over them, and wrings his hapless hands, and trembling stands aloof while all is shared and all is borne away, ready to starve, and dare not touch his own."* (Shakespeare)

The willingness of South African Jews to repay with contempt the privileges and opportunities of citizenship in one of the richest (and freest) countries of the world, to which most of them fled as penniless refugees, has caused them to be widely hated.

It is not generally believed, however, that they will stay to enjoy the fruits of black rule when it comes; at that point it will become the moral duty of some other country, perhaps one even richer and more generous than South Africa, to take them in on the grounds of their religion and give them another chance.

The Rhodesians will have no such privilege. Their passports are only recognized by South Africa and Switzerland. Stay and be slaughtered.

Britain, which only recently modified a law theoretically permitting any citizen of a Commonwealth Country (that is, about half the world) to enter Britain as a permanent resident regardless of money, skills, diseases or knowledge of English, will take black Rhodesians, but not the white.

Stay and be slaughtered. Why should they negotiate? They know that as long as white authority is maintained, they are safe; but the day it crumbles, their homes will be attacked, their wives will be raped, and their children will be butchered.

This is no fantasy; it has happened in a dozen UN member states. It is dismissed as fantasy by people who live in fantasies of their own.

There are people in Rhodesia who fled as refugees twice already, who have fled from country – from Goa – to Mozambique or Angola – to Rhodesia – from Kenya or Tanzania – to Zambia – to Rhodesia – from Germany, or China, or Lithuania – to Rhodesia...

Do you see something happening to the map?

– Algeria, Somalia, Mozambique, Angola, Cape Verde, Viet Nam, the Canal, the other Canal, the Cape;

– The Mediterranean, the Persian Gulf, the Indian Ocean, the South Atlantic, the South Pacific;

– All the world's shipping, all the world's waterways, all the world's oceans; all the world's oil, all the world's gold, all the world's chrome, all the world's natural resources.

Let the Americans believe it does not matter if the world is controlled by their enemies. Let them learn.

Let them learn when it is too late.

What will you do? Will you have the courage of the Rhodesians?

UDI began with a quote from Shakespeare:

"That he which hath no stomach to this fight, let him depart. He today that sheds his blood with me, shall be my brother, and gentlemen in England, now a-bed, shall think themselves accursed they were not here."

Will it end with another?

"A dream of what thou wert; a breath, a bubble, a sign of dignity, A garish flag to be the aim of every dangerous shot... Having naught but the thought of what thou wert, To torture you the more, being what thou art. Come, lead me to the block; bear them my head. They smile at me that shortly shall be dead."

Rhodesian rape bait (right) awaiting the joys of "majority rule" (left).

Overweight "exploited" Africans line up to vote for majority rule, 1979, followed, in many cases, by emigration to Britain or flight to South Africa. The "majority" today would probably emigrate anywhere they could, now that they have their "rule". Thanks.

Bibliography

Books: *Rhodesia Accuses* by A.J.A. Peck; *Call Africa 999* by John Peer Nugent; *The Fabric of Terror* by Bernardo Teixeira; *Traitor's End* by Nathaniel Weyl; *The Terror Fighters* by Al J. Venter; *Tuez-les tous!* by Jean Buhler; *White Man, Think Again!* by A. Jacobs; and a wide variety of other books on Africa, particularly *Inside Africa* by John Gunther.

Newspapers: *London Daily Telegraph*; *Los Angeles Times*; *Human Events*; a wide variety of American and British conservative newsletters, particularly the newsletter of the Christian Anti-Communist Crusade, edited by Dr. Fred Schwarz of Long Beach California; a number of Rhodesian, South African and Portuguese newspapers and magazines, particularly *To the Point* and *Property & Finance* (Salisbury). The last was destroyed in a libel action by Ian Smith the day after the editor's only son was killed in action fighting a no-win war at the behest of the sell-out Smith government.

At a public meeting a few days later, there was a shout: *"What about the paralyzed soldiers in St. Giles' Hospital?"* The answer (given, not by Smith, but by Smith's chief flunky, "Boss" Lilford, a tobacco millionaire, later murdered on his farm): *"They will just have to take their chances."*

Good luck. Shortly after the "independence" of Mozambique in 1974, a Portuguese woman gave birth to a baby in a Portuguese-built hospital in the capital city of Beira, Mozambique, now Maputo, assisted by an African, by all accounts a fully-qualified physician. The delivery was successful and apparently without difficulty, after which the black doctor simply took the newborn baby and drowned it in a basin or sink right in front of the horrified mother, saying, *"There are too many white babies in the world"*!

This is what you get for curing all their filthy diseases and sending them to medical school. This is what you get for teaching Africans to read. So much for the myth of the *"educated African"*.

This text is offered for what it is worth. Readers who do not believe in the reality of the African atrocities described herein are invited to substitute a few African atrocities of their own choosing. The text is so far out of date (almost 40 years old) that necklacing hadn't even been invented yet.

Epilogue

I was in Rhodesia in 1973, and was married in South Africa. The above were my impressions, written in the United States in 1976 and widely distributed by Dr. W. Steuart McBirnie and Roland L. Morgan, both of them Evangelical Christians.

It contains certain predictions about the future. Was I right or wrong? Well, I was wrong in predicting that the Mashona would be exterminated by the Matabele. With the help of 15,000 troops from North Korea, it was more or less the other way around. Anything else?

In most ways, the situation is worse than I expected, or ever dreamed possible. I expected the continent to be taken over by the Chinese, but I expected the Chinese to keep the Africans in order (or exterminate them).

Instead, the Africans, after destroying dozens of prosperous, modern countries in what is incomparably the richest continent on Planet Earth – since even the desert regions are blessed or cursed with immense untapped mineral resources – *these same Africans* are now breeding exponentially by the hundreds of millions, thanks solely to white charity, and are emigrating, legally or illegally, to European countries to escape a "poverty and misery" entirely of their own making – a process which would, if permitted, put an end to civilization as certainly, completely and permanently as thermonuclear warfare.

Today Detroit, tomorrow the world.

Oddly, when we are told to "*Save the Children*", we are shown skeletal African children with bony limbs and pot bellies.

But when we are told to "*Help the Asylum Seekers*", we are shown muscular, well-fed Africans in fashionable sports clothes, loaded down with cell phones and other electronic junk. Their illegal boat "tickets" cost €2,500 each, payable – cash down – to the Mafia.

And who masterminds these things? Who orchestrates these endless appeals for pity? Why, the same people who destroyed South Africa – the Jews! *The same people* who openly declare Israel "*a Jewish State*", surrounded by a 25-foot-high "*Wall of Separation*", with concentration camps in the hot desert sun for African "*asylum seekers*" of their own, while telling us to do the exact opposite! And we do. Is there any limit to white idiocy?

I know South African white refugees in Europe today who have lost everything, in Rhodesia and South Africa both, and *they are still liberals*. No matter how many necklacings, voodoo mutilation murders, rapes, and torture cases occur in their immediate area, no matter how many times they are attacked, no matter how many times they lose everything they own, *they never learn*.

In Hitler's words, "Those who do not wish to fight in this world of eternal struggle, do not deserve to live." *Vae victis!*

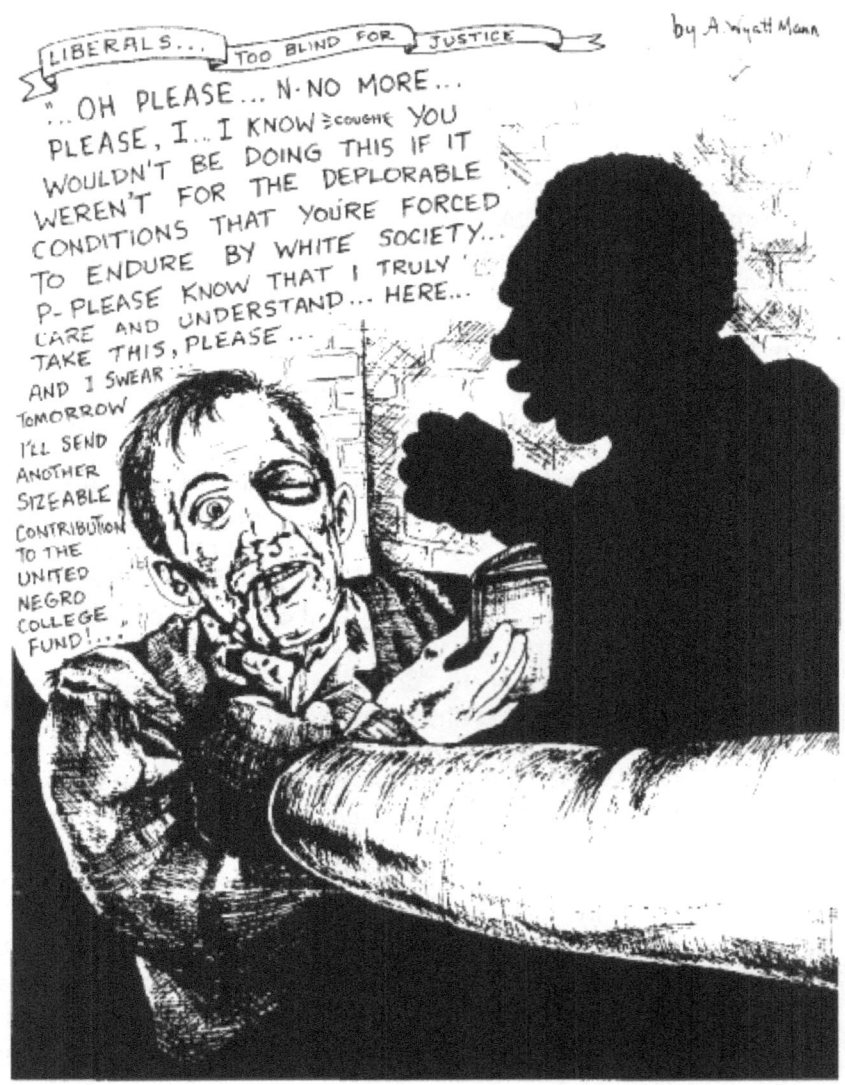

Cartoon by A. WYATT MANN.

Carlos Whitlock Porter

www.cwporter.com

www.ingramcontent.com/pod-product-compliance
Lightning Source LLC
LaVergne TN
LVHW041552060526
838200LV00037B/1256